THE FIRST
doo-lally
daft blinkin'
bonkers
book

FOR TONY, NED, ARTIE
AND MY BARKING MAD FAMILY ON
BOTH SIDES OF THE PLANET.

KEEP LAUGHING!

X

THE FIRST doo-lally daft blinkin' bonkers book

AINSLEY WAITE

upstart press

what do you give a sick PIG?

what do you call a SPIDER with NO LEGS?

a...

CURRANT.

why did the TOILET PAPER ROLL down the hill?

to get to the BOTTOM.

why was afraid 6 of 7?

KNOCK, KNOCK...

who's there?

BOO!

boo who...?!

THERE'S no need to cry, it's ONLY a joke!

what's a GHOST'S favourite dessert?

Doctor, doctor, Everyone's ignoring me...

why did the HEDGEHOG CROSS the road...?

to see **HIS** FLATMATE...!

hOw do yOu make A SAUSAGE ROLL?

PUSH
it down a hill!

what's Yellow AND DANGEROUS?

SHARK-
INFESTED
CUSTARD.

Why does the ocean ROAR...?

Wouldn't **you** if **you** had **crabs** on your **bottom**?!

what's RED and invisible?

No tomatoes!

what do you get if you dial 00640987248113067396524...

a BIG
blister
ON YOUR
FINGER...!

what's

BROWN

and

Sticky?

Doctor, doctor, I THINK I need glasses...

I agree. THIS is the Post OFFICE.

what's yellow and AND STUPID...?

thick
CUSTARD.

KNOCK, KNOCK... who's there?

banana!

banana who?

KNOCK, KNOCK... who's there?

banana!

banana who?

KNOCK, KNOCK...

who's there?

Orange!

orange who...?!

orange you glad I Didn'T say banana!

why did the crab go to JAIL?

'coz it kept

PINCHING

stuff!

what do you call a FLY with NO WINGS?

a....

WALK.

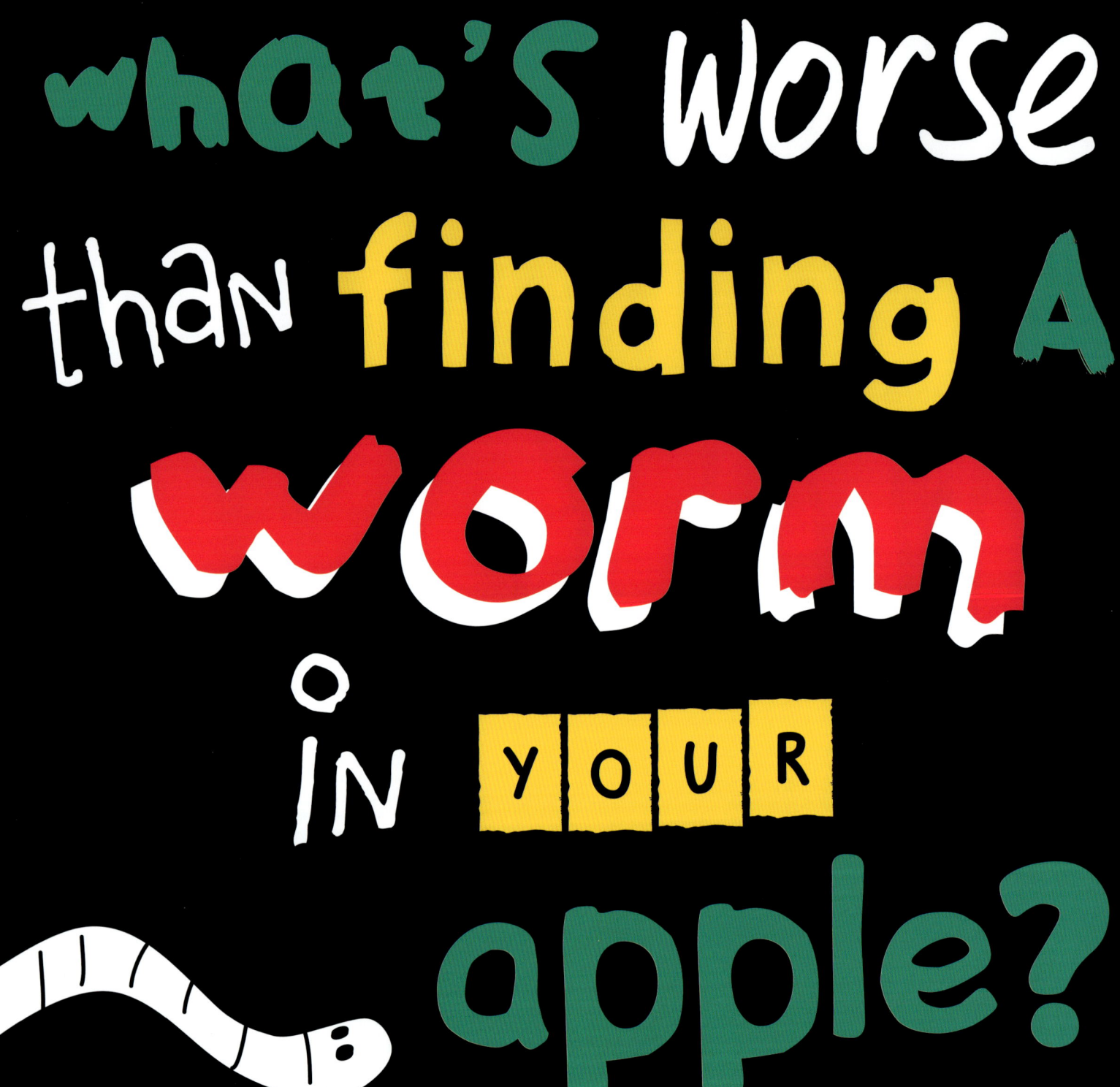

finding HALF A worm!

what's BIG, has wheels and FLIES?

a...

rubbish

TRUCK!

what's the FASTEST cake in the world?

...SCONE!

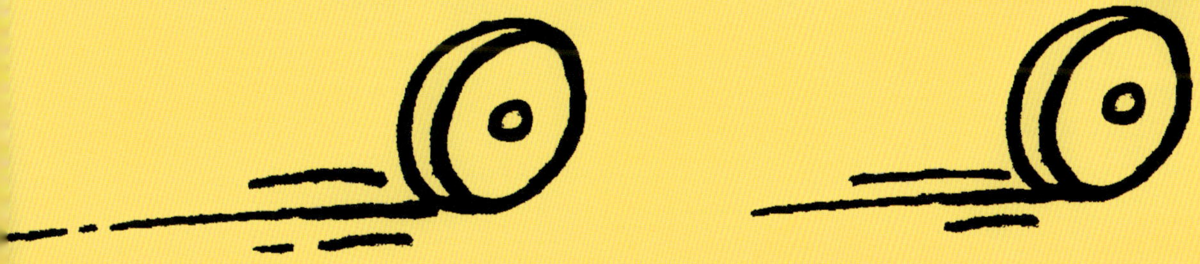

what's the second fastest cake in the world?

..MERRRINGUE!

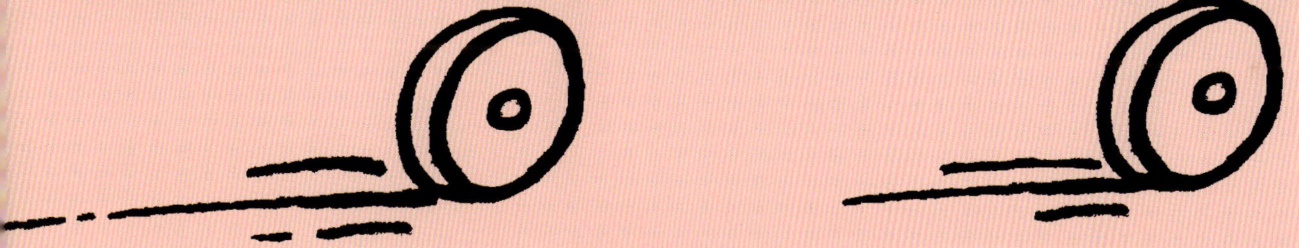

what's BROWN and sounds like A BELL?

KNOCK, KNOCK....

who's there?

toodle.

toodle who...?!

good
bye!

A catalogue record for this book is available
from the National Library of New Zealand

ISBN 978-1-988516-89-9

An Upstart Press Book
Published in 2019 by Upstart Press Ltd
Level 6, BDO Tower, 19-21 Como St, Takapuna 0622
Auckland, New Zealand

Printed by Everbest Printing Co. Ltd., China